IN A RIND OF LIGHT

IN A RIND OF LIGHT

Catherine Abbey Hodges

STEPHEN F. AUSTIN STATE UNIVERSITY PRESS

For information about permission to reproduce selections from this book, contact *permissions* :

Stephen F. Austin State University Press
P.O. Box 13007, SFA Station
Nacogdoches, TX 75962
sfapress@sfasu.edu
www.sfasu.edu/sfapress
936-468-1078

Project Manager: Kimberly Verhines
Cover art: *Into the Unknown,* Hermon Atkins MacNeil, c. 1912
Photo credit: Mim Abbey
Author photo: Rob Hodges

ISBN: 978-1-62288-305-9

For you
in your rind of light

CONTENTS

*To witness fully and be thus
the altar of the thing witnessed.*

– Ursula K. LeGuin

You may board at either end of Childhood.

– Li-Young Lee

OR MAYBE IT'S MORE LIKE THIS
— after Wislawa Szymborska

The child who sits
              on the braided rug
       watching the waves

while the others sleep
             through the growing light

          is growing a self of sand,
salted wind, skein of kelp,
    last stars. Soon

          she'll give her self a new name,
one that means Window
      in a language she makes as she goes.

I

ALL PARTICLE, ALL WAVE

Here you're dying and all
I can think of is birth
        and how you are,
as ever, more

than meets the eye: both
laboring mother and stubborn
infant laboring too,
        tunneling toward

what isn't wheeling
seagulls, not a hammered silver
        bay—toward what's nothing
I can name:

so much everything
        and all at once,
                all particle, all wave.

IT'S A PEWTER AFTERNOON

in a distant city—whether distant
in miles or time doesn't matter,
though it's both. What matters is someone
is leaving and someone arriving.
Someone is falling down the stairs,
a baby in her arms.

                She's bruised
and scraped when the landing breaks
her fall. The baby, unharmed, won't
remember this. The woman's
ankle will never
forget.

      One day she'll tell this story. Later,
the one who was the baby that day
will make a song of it:

        the stairs, the arms, the ankle. The fall
down the days, the clatter, the landing.
The stairs, the arms, the days.
The fall, the falling,
the arms.

THREE MONTHS AFTER YOUR DEATH

What's falling now has come from far away—
the Ganges or some icy childhood lake.
I know, I know: *far* is likely one more
of my exaggerations. And *away*'s less

precise than *within*. You and your devotion
to accuracy. What's falling
now has come from . . .
1963? The other side of this blue

door? Here's the thing: my eyes
ache, the lilacs are abuzz about some
private arrangement they've made with you,
the sky's still putting its prehistoric question

to the lichen which turns away and tells the old
story to the stone, and something keeps pouring
me from now into after or before, spilling me
from far away to here to far away.

MY MOTHER'S HANDS

What lasts depends
on who you ask
I used to think.
Now I think who's to say,
since look at us,
our manifest unlastingness,
this knack for vanishing.

Still, if on pain
of something dear
I had to make a list today:

Flash of needle
in brisk young fingers,
draw and tug of yellow thread.

Those fingers (coral nails)
striking a match to light
a Coleman stove,
sudden bloom
in early autumn dusk.

And further back,
strong hands, fingers splayed,
lifting a slick child
from a tub,
bundling her in turquoise,
holding her (I feel
as if I'm flying)
to watch the little whirlpool

dance above the drain
as the sudsy water
glugs out, lasting
as anything.

THE VISIT

It was summer
and too early
to go to bed
but I was in bed
and my sister
came in
and climbed
under the sheet
with me.

We were
at our parents'
house, visiting,
in our thirties,
the window
open,
the dusty lace
curtains rising
and falling
with the breeze.

"Mom told me
something,"
said my sister.
I had no idea
what she would
say next.
"She told me it
happened to her.
She said it
was Granddaddy."
The curtains rose

and fell,
rose and fell.

I couldn't breathe

and then I could

though now
it was different:
the air, my lungs,
everything.

TWO RED SWEATERS

I've been squinting
all evening at our
grainy arms and legs,
our eyes, our mouths
in the hours transferred
from Super 8 (tick tick tick)
to video to DVD,
looking for portents,
any hint at all,
the slightest foreshadowing
of your disappearance,
still decades off,
and finding none,
just our supple, smiling
parents and our leggy
selves darting self-conscious
glances at the future
which lay hidden as June
foothills in coastal fog.
But here's something,
maybe: long minutes
of the swollen Kern River
rushing away—
footage I can picture Dad
shooting as our frugal
mother admonished him
to *Save the film*
for what will matter
years from now
(us, she meant), as if
there'd always be that river
hurtling past a campsite

we'd never forget
(though I'd forgotten
it till tonight),
as if we wouldn't
want—need—the record
of its swift passage
now that you're
on the far bank
slipping away
between granite rocks
in the smaller of those red
sweaters Mom knit, one
for me, one for you . . .
and all of a sudden
I remember
the celluloid ribbon
spilling off the reel
one night in 1974,
pouring in loose loops
onto the green shag carpet
before Dad hit the off button,
flipped the lights back on
to see what had gone
wrong.

THE GIFT

After my mother's death,
friends spoke of her gift
for disregarding
her own needs,
as if this were a talent
and not a scar
from an old,
old wound.

Near the end, though,
as she lay jaundiced
and furrow-browed
in pink sheets,
I offered her
a sip of water
and she opened
her mouth—not
to speak (she'd sailed out
past speech), but,
it seemed to me,
to consult her body
at last.

Then she had
her answer
and made a tight seam
with her lips.

Anyone watching
would have mistaken
my sudden tears
for grief.

THE LAST DAY

Now that you're gone, ashes
in a box on Dad's closet shelf
in an apartment you never saw,
I'm letting myself get to know you
better.
      Today, for instance,
it occurred to me to imagine you
on the last day of your childhood,
and once I thought of it, I couldn't
look away.
      You were seven, maybe
eight, that last day before your father
stole those years of days when
your worst pain should have been
a skinned knee or disappointing
grade,
      your best-kept secret the gift
you were making your mother
for Christmas—her cross-stitch
initial on the handkerchief
you bought with coins
you saved from your
birthday money.
      Can you blame me,
Mom? I need that last day as much
as I've ever needed anything, need
to see you in it, then put
that to rest too.

OWL-SHAPED ABSENCE

Yesterday morning I saw in the old oak,
the one I worry about every winter before
it leafs out again in the spring, a pygmy owl.

It sat so still that I wouldn't have noticed it
except that all around it tiny birds piped and flitted,
the sun catching the tips of their wings
and their throats. They drew my attention
as they would have yours, Mom, and then I saw
the other bird. From where I stood on the deck,
we were eye level with each other. Forty feet
or so away, it perched, alert, as if waiting
for me to find it.

Once I did, I wasn't sure what I was looking at.
It was broad daylight, so *owl* wasn't my first guess,
but a long look through the binoculars (thank you
for those, among other things) and then
Peterson's *Field Guide to Western Birds*
persuaded me.

There it stayed for several hours, motionless
save for the occasional swivel of its head.

Each time I looked the owl's direction, through
the window or from the deck, it seemed to me
that across the distance, eyes I knew and didn't know
were on me. When I lowered my head,
I still felt their gaze.

Then I got caught up in the day's work—oh how my
industry impressed all the grown-ups of my childhood
but you, and how little I've unlearned—
and when I looked out some time
after 3:00, the bird was gone.

This morning it hasn't returned. Wet grasses
and fallen leaves glisten in the brilliant winter light,
and in the oak where the pygmy owl spent yesterday,
I now find a small vacancy. Sunlit, owl-shaped
absence. Emptiness with room
for comings and goings.

IN MY DREAM OUR MOTHER IS STILL MAKING LINOLEUM BLOCK CHRISTMAS CARDS

She bends over a snowflake with her silver blade
and they blossom, intricate flock,
while a brilliant partridge

sets up oil paint, brayer, glass plate of strange
birds at rest in a pear tree. She rolls out the paint
on an eastern skyline in the twilit kitchen:

hundreds in flight, cityscape
with domes and minarets. Later
she reads us stories, tucks us into bed inside

the clocks, behind the gears and rubies. We wake
to windowsills thick with wings—fresh prints
from near and far, melting fast.

THE NEXT DREAM

In the next dream, having slept inside the clocks,
we wake in the dark and mess with the gears.
I pry some rubies free and pocket them—
my plan, of course, to hock them, buy more time.

PSALM FOR THE SPILL, THE POUR

In distant meadows and in fields beside the highway

    horses in their bright pour

        their glossy spill

            toward particle and wave

                lift their heads.

                    We all do.

                    We are each other's witnesses.

II

SONG OF THE HINGE

At Fantastic Sam's a while back,
      sitting in the chair, looking at myself
            looking back from the mirror, my hair falling

           to the shiny floor, for no particular reason
     I can remember I asked the young woman
with the scissors what she liked most

about her job. She thought for a moment—
      snip snip—and then said *I love the sound*
            of the scissors. Ever since then, I've thought

         about the sounds of a vocation, wondered
    if love of those could be a kind of measure:
have you found your true work?

Do you love its sounds? Lighthouse keepers,
      your foghorns? Violinists, the snap
         of your case, opening? Jockeys, the stomp

         and nicker? I have no idea what I'm talking about,
    of course, except when I'm speaking of myself,
and then in part at best. Speaking of myself,

for myself, I love the scritch scritch
      of a room of students writing. Not typing,
         or keyboarding as we say these days, but pen-

         to-paper, hand-moving-across-the-page writing,
    a sound that I associate with a second sound
as the result of a dream.

In this dream I had a giant
      pad of paper—taller than me—
         and I understood that my task was to write

in it, fill it up. So I did, filled the first page
with words from top to bottom, then reached
to turn the page which, in that moment, turned

into a door. If I walked through, I brought
no memory of that back from the dream,
but ever since, the textured sound of many

writers writing makes me think of the sounds
a door makes as it opens: click of latch, squeak
of hinge. It's 10:30 in the morning,

7:45 in the evening, and we're bent to the page,
thirty of us, filling it up, writing our doors. I have
less than no idea what their doors

will open on, or mine for that matter,
when the latch clicks, when the hinge
sings its small song.

GLOSA ON LINES FROM PETER EVERWINE

In the vacant lot, a common thrush
picks his way through a maze of rubble,
searching for something to fill himself
before he sings.

Poet, you're in the ground
and I'm wearing your vest
for luck, solace, magic . . .
for I don't know what. So far
it's working for warmth.
I can say that much
on this cold day at my desk,
all grey out the window, and inside
a dim winter hush.
In the vacant lot, a common thrush

pulls my gaze past the dusty pane
to where he flits and hops, intent.
He's lively and precise.
How can he be so nimble
while I sit here dim as my room,
this dull morning's double?
And just like that, here comes
envy—of a bird! A common bird
that, unconcerned with my muddle,
picks his way through a maze of rubble

(an odd place for a thrush, it seems
to me, though you're the one who put
or found him there in your poem,
and he's free to leave this one but hasn't
yet). He's absorbed in his work,
so far as I can tell—

flitting, hopping with a flare
of wing, flick of tail,
foraging without our help,
searching for something to fill himself

which is what I'll need to do too,
though not yet. I'm not done with this
brimming emptiness.
Here in your vest, I'm full
of what's gone, picking through what's left,
listening for whatever will bring
whatever's next. And now that bird
darts a glance straight at me, now
looks away, flares his wings
before he sings.

TITLE ENVY

Blue autumn
when the big wind comes
     like a soprano
in the hour between dog and wolf
and a hundred million years of nectar dances:
     bright dead things.
After west
we almost disappear.

There's a ghost in this machine of air
listening long and late
     happy in an ordinary thing
        given sugar, given salt.
Queen of a rainy country,
say this prayer into the past.

AT DUSK THE CHILDREN

– after Wolf Kahn's *Barn Silhouette*

At dusk the children don't come home.
All day they've ridden easy
on the mare in her mind
but when dusk comes
barn door open
dust undisturbed
then she knows
she's set too many
places at the table again, knows
the soup on the stove will last the week.
The light over the sink throws its cold square
on the yard. Nothing shifts in the barn all night.

EMPTY PLACES

– after Van Gogh's Street in Auvers-sur-Oise

I don't want to know what the art historians think about Van
Gogh's *Street in Auvers-sur-Oise* with its unfinished sky above
the orange roofs and the flickering greens of the plane trees. I
want to think of Van Gogh gone shy in the face of heaven, this
time not sure it's his to paint the mystery lifting away from or
rinsing down on the village, leaving it a suggestion in cerulean
and empty canvas.

And the canvas is a window.   Behind the glass,   looking
in through the   empty places, some   being,
familiar and   other as a   recurring   dream,
overcome by absent   detail: pigeon on a roof,
snapped sunflower   stalk, shadow in a   doorway,   pail
of milk.   She presses f i n g e r s   to the   window
through which she regards not   just these but   the
artist,   the villagers and their chickens, the experts I
decline to consult,   all of us, from her lonely nimbus   of
rainlight.

SEPTEMBER TARANTULA

I met her on the trail today,
furred and fleshed like me, her
steps delicate in the glint of sun
off granite and oak light's dusty filter,

neither of us in a hurry.
Streaks of quartz like lightning
in a boulder just up hill mirrored
the contrails overhead, minerals and vapors

fraying to oblivion in their own time
while she and I regarded one another.

At length, we blessed each other
on our solitary ways, in the wisdoms

of our bodies:
hail, sister, and fare well.

LATE OCTOBER, MIDDLE FORK

From the high far bank

    where the wild grapes

        have purpled on their vines

            and the figs that remain

      now that foxes and thrashers

        have feasted

            fall at intervals

      like great drops of rain

            into the dark-bright swirl,

     grape leaves

        and fig leaves

            drift down—festival

         lanterns—

            toward their own

                  lit faces.

RAIN FELL THROUGH THE NIGHT

Rain fell through the night
and this morning the river's bounding
like a pack of hounds on a scent.
They're baying like bells
and remind me of me,
on the trail, as well,
of something wild—
more wildness
for my grief?
If I corner it, will
I wolf it down?
Bad form for a hound,
but maybe then I'd spend
this sorrow faster, wash the salt
out of my eyes, off my skin, out
of my hair. Is that what I need?
What if the hounds turn out to be
horses, pounding past? What if I vault
up onto a sorrel, do no more than hold on,
ride all the way to the sea.

GOLDEN SHOVEL AT THE END OF A YEAR

There is in me, always,
you and the absence of you.
        – Peter Everwine

From here I see the river glint there
through the sycamores. It is
dark with ash from autumn's fires in
the mountains. The old year has broken me
into many pieces. I am always
hearing you and you and you
in the wind hymning through the pines and
in Orion's shining silences. The
way you gone ones spin absence
into light is the better part of
my reassembly at the workbench of life after you.

III

LATE AFTERNOON MEDITATION ON AN OPEN EGG CARTON

Light slips like water off an egg
and pools in the carton's empty rooms,
goes where it wants to go, does what it wants to . . .

follows its own lights, so to speak.
Why did I ascribe, right there, volition to light?
Do I mean, instead, vocation? Not what light *wants*

to do but what *calls* to it? Volition, vocation—what
am I, a dictionary? All I know
is that at times I aspire to nothing

more than to slip from the world's surfaces
the way light slips off hoods of semis,
Half Dome, spoons, eggs. The way

it crested, then slid from, the cheek
of my firstborn, my lastborn's brow, my mother's
face the morning she didn't wake, and pooled elsewhere.

GOODBYE THISTLE

Six a.m. and already bees
are at it like frenzied babies
at the breast, ravishing the powdered
nipples of the Matilija poppies.

She thinks of milky mornings
with one baby, another.
None with the one in between. The two:
frantic mouths, then eyes rolled back, elemental hour.
Warm bodies against hers, heavier by day, by week.
The one: lighter by year, weight of ash,
pollen heft, always there.

Memory's hall, flooded now with early light,
is full and never filled. Through windows,
breezes come and go, sparrows. In the pouring
brightness, motes eddy and swirl, pollen
from the thistle of goodbye.

I WHO NEVER

You're dying and I
who never get hangnails
have a hangnail.

Where are you going?
Where did my childhood go?
Where is that light now?

I know. If it's anywhere,
it's in me. I know.
I'm dying too.

CRADLE

The night before I picked up your ashes,
the wind was fierce and I was awake
for what felt like hours listening

to the branches thrash outside my window.
At last I slept, and in the morning, for the first
time in years, I woke in my childhood

bedroom in full daylight, in the camphor tree
with bark like the skin of an old giant,
the glossy leaves, the cradle of branches.

I CAN'T REMEMBER IF I'VE TOLD YOU

that the day you died
a giraffe was born at the zoo
four miles away. I'm sorry

I let it drive me crazy
that you always
had to warm the plates

before you served dinner.
I'm sorry I never
let you curl my hair.

PRAISE WHAT LASTS PAST FLAME

Praise what's gone
the one who takes it
praise the match
the one who strikes it

praise the tinder
ghosts of grasses
air epistle
hymn of smoke.

Praise what burns
what keeps on burning
praise the things
that last past flame

blackened key
I'll scour to gleaming
shard of pane I'll
polish, keep.

SOFT SHOULDER

reads the sign on Highway 99.
The sky's a thirsty violet
and fields of bleached stubble
extend on either side,
and now there's no shoulder
at all for so long
that although we don't speak of it
we both feel stalked
by a narrowing
that starts on the road
then moves inside
to the car's stale air
and further inside to our arteries,
capillaries, thread-bare
yearnings, the idea
of self at last so narrow,
compressed,
all that's left is a buzz
or wave of sound
or light that meets the pulsing
sky
in an exchange
we will never speak of
because we won't know how
before the construction ends
and the road widens.

SWEET PEAS ON THE DASH

We're a cross between our parents
and hippies in a tent.
— Greg Brown

We'll sell the silver, buy an old truck,
plant sweet peas and cantaloupe.
We'll tend and harvest. Mend.
It's a highway's what it is
even when we're home.

Hours are miles, days
are fields of something blue
that smells like childhood.
Nights are hills on hills and horses
under a moon always
blooming gibbous.

We roll the windows down.
Sweet peas on the dash, melons
in the bed, radio belting our song.

I HEART YOU

since who am I to say the word
that should burn my tongue, singe
the air as it leaves
my lips?

I muscle and blood you,
I pound you and glisten
and throb you,
pump blood

all the way to your coasts. O
let's heart one another
so fierce and so true
all our consonants melt into vowels.

RADIANCE IN THE AMPLITUHEDRON

*In 2013, Nima Arkani-Hamed and Jaroslav Trnka discovered
a reformulation of scattering amplitudes that makes reference to
neither space nor time. They found that the amplitudes of certain
particle collisions are encoded in the volume of a jewel-like
geometric object, which they dubbed the amplituhedron.*
— Natalie Wolchover, *The New Yorker*

Here inside the amplituhedron
I'm eating a corned beef sandwich on rye
without reference to space or time

and let me tell you: it tastes
amazing. This must be what I've waited
for my whole life and what

I was looking for with all that education,
knitting, meditation, Burning Man,
regular church attendance.

Everything here is, naturally, ample,
and then there's the radiance—all those grains
of scattered light, colliding and, well, *radiant,*

which is scattering amplitude code (slang,
really) for the spirit's volume as it
enters or leaves a body.

ON A WARM APRIL TUESDAY

The deluxe box of new crayons in stadium seating,

    the radish-puller pointing the way with a radish,

oxalis and mustard pouring through fences,

    the ice cream truck with its garbled wake

of children, its immortal tuneless tune: here we are,

    here in this grainy four p.m., this loose-limbed

life, fleck of heaven, me in love all over.

A SPELL FOR WHAT COMES NEXT

The ice plant grew along the edges of the playground so that
we could break off the fleshy leaves and use them—the original magic
markers—to write spells on the asphalt. We cast spells for boys
to talk to us, spells to trip the fastest kid on the other
kickball team. The "ink" was mostly water the plant had evolved
to store for survival and incantations of skinny girls in the 1970s.

When the spell was, say, longer than three words of three
letters each, and when the day was hot or even warm, the first letter
evaporated before the last was complete—the original disappearing
ink. We were disappearing, too, into longer legs, the beginnings
of breasts, the spells of the 70s and 80s—love work children
work love yes love, an enchantment from which I'm just now waking,
stretching, sitting up, blinking into the strange wind-scoured light.
Where am I, and where is my ice plant? Don't make me ask again.

IV

WE FIND HONEY OTHERS MISS

reads the H&R Block sign.
It's April of course and I'm charmed
by this as I am by the scrawl of early lilacs

in the alley. Even when I realize
I've mistaken an *M* for an *H*, it's a slip
neither Freud nor I mind, a mistake I'm

happy to have made.
Decades, really, of error and blunder
are how I've found honey

in the least likely places,
where bees had no business, and how,
eating it raw by the spoonful

or sucking it straight from the comb,
I've gone places I had no business going.
My dear

mistakes are how I found my life.

IF YOU'RE A BOOK

I'm told that when I was very young
I'd strip the dust jackets from books
first thing. Me at two, three, four
in a world before board books, opening
gifts on my birthday, frowning, pulling
the Caldecott-winning covers right off.

I have no memory of this, and my parents
never explained, only offered it
as evidence that I knew what I wanted
from the get-go.

I still don't want anything
to come between me and the words, the life
on the page. I scribble scolds, swoons,
questions, nods all over the margins.
And I dog-ear. I've dog-eared for years
where the words have floored me,
slain and saved me. I love the bend,
the fold, the crease that's left
like an intimate scar
if the fold is smoothed back.
This has lost me some respectability,
of course, and perhaps I should care,

but I don't. If you're a book, no matter
how attractive you look in that jacket,
what I want, still, is what's inside.
Later, we'll bear each other's marks
into the rest of our lives, each other's lives
into the rest of our own.

A CLEAR MOMENT

Today I looked up from my important lists and papers
into a memory of canyon light, of words in the river
and words in the trees that line its banks—

First Bank of the Cottonwoods, Second Church
of Sky, Our Lady of Sycamore Bark and her mottled
maps of time, her runic questions I haven't asked

since childhood. Hour by hour, as I'm at what a call my work,
those river-scented pages peel away and fall, enter
the loam beneath words, become it.

AT MORRO STRAND: SONG FOR WHAT RUNS TO THE SEA

Nasturtiums and ice plant spill over the cliff toward the sea.
      Maybe everything does in the end. Soon I'll move to a small house

on the middle fork of a river hundreds of miles inland—and this
      is where that river's headed, bearing flecks of mountain,

mineral byways of its surge and seep. It disappears
      in places, trades light for beetles, worms, roots of trees,

only to surface later with a new name and then another,
      and all those miles it's sea-fevered, ocean-bound.

Sitting on the sand this afternoon, watching the waves break,
      the gulls wheel, the fog blow past in shreds, leaving

most of what I don't understand in the ancient hands
      of the outgoing tide, I know, somehow, that I'm seeing it all,

and that there are no words for what I mean by this, or none
      I've found so far, and that I have no plans to stop looking.

NEXT WE'RE STANDING IN THE MOONLIGHT

Goodbye these creaky floors, this beveled
    early light through these panes, this bright
        bloom on the scarred hardwood, details
            we know by heart. Farewell,

goodbye. *What a beautiful little house,*
    writes Patrick. *I would never want to leave.*
        It's alright, friend, it's practice, rehearsal,
            a steady getting ready,

like playing scales, like hitting the tennis ball
    against the side of the school cafeteria
        through long June twilights. This morning
            on my walk, though, I met an old dog,

stopped to pat the shaggy head. She leaned,
    suddenly, against my legs, a firm pressing,
        and I felt the vibration I sometimes
            feel when I stand outdoors alone

for a long while, something
    sympathetic between the earth
        and the soles of my feet, and as
            clearly as if that dog had said so,

I knew: this isn't practice. Or it *is*
    practice and it's also the real deal,
        the two at the same time. We're
            rehearsing and it's opening night

of a one-night show. Here's the music
     from the pit, and we're on, we stumble
          through our lines, and it's over. Next
              we're standing in the moonlight,

shrugging on our coats, trying
     to remember what we've heard
          about the after party—where to find
              it, what we were supposed to bring

besides ourselves, besides each other,
     searching our memories
          for what that might mean, trusting
              in the end the not knowing is enough.

LITTLE INCARNATIONS

I'm watching a raven
in the high blue
glide
then tuck wings
and drop down the air
next pull out of her fall
with a deft sleight
of wing
and repeat.

I salute
her pinioned life
from here inside
my furred
one—
both of us little
incarnations of a crazy
notion, each of us
a yes.

MARY AND MARTHA

are having it out again in the kitchen of my heart
is what I used to think once I'd gotten past
the idea that I was one or the other of them
at any given time and swung from resentment
to sanctimony and back ad infinitum.

Now, though, we've found a kind of peace. Most days
we make breakfast together, gossip a little around
the blue table, eat what we've fixed. Silver
threads our hair. Sometimes friends

drop by, share news
and whatever's on the stove or in the fridge.
Out the window, some days, the breeze moves
the leaves a certain way and light falls like coins or rain.

Whatever we're doing or saying then, we stop for that.

SUNDAY MORNING IN THE CHURCH OF AIR

Sunday morning in the church of air,
great blue heron hunched over the good
book, chapters and verses swirling
about his legs.
Never the same river,
always the same word—history, proverb,
psalm, parable—and the one sermon
in many tongues season to season,
moment to moment, whether
I attend or not.
         Pews of lichened granite,
obsidian cherts that caught the light
before landing among the grasses
and fallen leaves:
the wood ducks
in the high windows know it all
by heart. Small birds with names
I don't recall
sound from sycamores
like bells.
        And none of this depends
on me, though I see now that somehow
I depend on it—the river, the stooped
heron and the one rising on great wings
above its reflection, the Yokuts family
at home here
in the ouzel's inner eyelid,
the wood ducks with their deep
memories
and the small birds

with their bells—
                  you and I depend
on this whether or not we've ever
darkened the slim doorway,
lifted the latch that's everywhere.

THIS THINNESS, THAT SPACE
 – for Peter Everwine, in memoriam

On the radio, an alto voice
sings *Time grows thin*
on descending notes,
stretching the *nnnnnnnn*
so that the dashboard
keeps buzzing
after the song's done.

Prince Wen Hui's cook,
wrote Chuang-Tzu,
told his dazzled master
his secret
for cutting up
an ox: Learn
the open places
between bone and bone,
bone and tendon,
ligament
and everything else.
Where this thinness—
the blade—*finds*
that space, there
is all the room you need,
explained the cook.

Some centuries later
in Kentucky,
after Thomas Merton
had translated Chuang-Tzu's
words, how could he

have been other
than under their influence
when he wrote
I am the appointed hour,
the 'now'
that cuts time
like a blade.

They're both gone,
of course, Chuang-Tzu
and Merton,
slipped into an opening
between what bones
I won't speculate, while
here inside my shred of life,
I'm learning
as hard as I can.

Last night in Fresno,
the 'now'
that slid gleaming
into time was the voice
of a poet, words
spoken like birds
into the deepening evening
where a scruffy crowd,
our faces shining
with traces
of barbequed chicken
and something harder
to name,
sat on blankets
and folding chairs

drinking boxed wine
from plastic cups.

The moon, descending
like a tusk on a thread,
gathered light,
the trees and grasses
collected dusk,
and there it was,
here it is—
space, found
and ample,
all the room I need.

EVEN THE POOREST THING

shines, wrote Layman P'ang, and so
it does. See how the bits of dead fly gleam
like peacock feathers and hummingbird throats,
these little chips of shine caught in the web
that softens the corner of the window. Truth is,

I came upon them while intent on swatting a living
fly buzzing in that window, a reflexive move,
and am now suffused with both confusion about
whether that part of the story belongs in this poem
and . . . not guilt, exactly, but a complicated sensation
that dogs my steps to the fridge and my reach

for a tub of blueberry yogurt, which also shines,
as does the spoon in the drawer I'm opening. And you
in the doorway, backlit, in your rind of light. You shine.
Forgive me if I'm only now saying so. You, the spoon,
the bright fly bits, the dried mud you're about to track in
and the fly it turns out I only stunned, up now
and bumbling the glass. Me too, I suppose,

all of us suspended in this hour's web:
here, poor, shining.

AUTHOR'S NOTES

"Glosa on Lines from Peter Everwine" is for Connie Lake. The epigraph is from the poem "156 Main Street." A form from the 14th century Spanish court, the *glosa* honors the work of another poet, taking a quatrain from that poet as a *cabeza* and ending each of the four ten-line stanzas with successive lines from the quatrain. Lines six and nine traditionally rhyme (mine slant a bit) with the final line in the stanza.

"Title Envy" is a cento, a poem composed entirely (or almost entirely) of found lines. This one is for the 14 poets whose book titles comprise it, with admiration and thanks.

"Golden Shovel at the End of a Year" is for Peter Everwine and Donna Alderson Abbey. The epigraph is from the poem "Elegiac Fragments." The Golden Shovel is a form invented by Terrence Hayes to honor Gwendolyn Brooks, the name referring to the "Seven at the Golden Shovel" of Brooks' "We Real Cool." Hayes' tribute poem places each word of her poem at the end of successive lines of his—and then does it again, in reverse order! (Nothing that ambitious happens in this one.)

"Radiance in the Amplituhedron" takes its epigraph from Natalie Wolchover's article "A Different Kind of Theory of Everything."

"On a Warm April Tuesday" borrows the radish puller from a poem by Issa, translated by Robert Hass:

> The man pulling radishes
> pointed the way
> with a radish.

ACKNOWLEDGMENTS

My thanks to the editors of the following publications, in which a number of the poems in this book first appeared or are forthcoming, some in earlier versions or under different titles:

The American Journal of Poetry: "Or Maybe It's More Like This," "Three Months after Your Death," "Two Red Sweaters"

Atticus Review: "All Particle, All Wave," "Goodbye Thistle," "I Heart You," "Soft Shoulder," "Title Envy"

Chicago Quarterly Review: "Even the Poorest Thing"

Levan Humanities Review: "It's a Pewter Afternoon"

Miramar: "Glosa on Lines from Peter Everwine"

Nimrod: "Late Afternoon Meditation on an Open Egg Carton"

ONE/Jacar Press: "Praise What Lasts Past Flame"

The Packinghouse Review: "At Dusk the Children"

A Spell for What Comes Next (Miramar Editions): "A Clear Moment," "If You're a Book," "In My Dream My Mother Is Still Making Linoleum Block Christmas Cards," "Little Incarnations," "At Morro Strand: Song for What Runs to the Sea," "Next We're Standing in the Moonlight," "A Spell for What Comes Next," "We Find Honey Others Miss"

SWWIM: "Sunday Morning in the Church of Air"

Writing Sound: "Song of the Hinge"

"Even the Poorest Thing" and "Sunday Morning in the Church of Air" also appeared in *A Spell for What Comes Next*.

A number of the poems in this collection became their better selves thanks to suggestions from Christopher Buckley, David Dominguez, Peter Everwine, Marie Howe, and Maggie Smith. I'm deeply grateful to each.

Warm thanks to Kimberly Verhines and Jerri Bourrous of Stephen F. Austin State University Press for skillful literary midwifery.

And thanks forever to Rob, Clara, and Mac Hodges.

ABOUT THE AUTHOR

CATHERINE ABBEY HODGES is the author of two previous poetry collections: *Instead of Sadness*, selected by Dan Gerber as winner of the 2015 Barry Spacks Poetry Prize, and *Raft of Days* (2017), both from Gunpowder Press. Her poems have been featured on *The Writer's Almanac* and *Verse Daily* and appear in venues including *The Southern Review, The American Journal of Poetry, Miramar, Chicago Quarterly Review, Connotation Press, SWWIM, Tar River Poetry* and *Atticus Review.* Named 2017 Faculty of the Year at Porterville College, Catherine mentors student writers, coordinates California Poets in the Schools for Tulare County, and collaborates with her husband, musician and labyrinth-maker Rob Hodges. Visit www.catherineabbeyhodges.com for more info.

CPSIA information can be obtained
at www.ICGtesting.com
Printed in the USA
BVHW081932060220
571676BV00001B/11